Stealing Man's Greatest Blessings

Stealing Man's Greatest Blessings

War on the Unborn

Adeline M. Cho

STEALING MAN'S GREATEST BLESSINGS
WAR ON THE UNBORN

Scripture quotations marked TPT are from The Passion Translation®. Copyright © 2017, 2018, 2020 by Passion & Fire Ministries, Inc. Used by permission. All rights reserved. ThePassionTranslation.com.

Scripture quotations marked NLT are taken from the Holy Bible, New Living Translation, copyright © 1996, 2004, 2007. Used by permission of Tyndale House Publishers, Inc. Carol Stream, Illinois 60188. All rights reserved. Website

Scripture quotations marked KJV are from the Holy Bible, King James Version (Authorized Version). First published in 1611. Quoted from the KJV Classic Reference Bible, Copyright © 1983 by The Zondervan Corporation.

Scripture quotations marked AMP are from The Amplified Bible, Old Testament copyright © 1965, 1987 by the Zondervan Corporation. The Amplified Bible, New Testament copyright © 1954, 1958, 1987 by The Lockman Foundation. Used by permission. All rights reserved.

Unless otherwise indicated, all scripture quotations are from The Holy Bible, English Standard Version® (ESV®). Copyright ©2001 by Crossway Bibles, a division of Good News Publishers. Used by permission. All rights reserved.

iUniverse books may be ordered through booksellers or by contacting:

iUniverse
1663 Liberty Drive
Bloomington, IN 47403
www.iuniverse.com
844-349-9409

ISBN: 978-1-6632-2185-8 (sc)
ISBN: 978-1-6632-2186-5 (e)

Library of Congress Control Number: 2021916671

Print information available on the last page.

iUniverse rev. date: 08/09/2021

To my precious Lord and Savior Jesus Christ, who, through the inspiration of the Holy Spirit, granted me this privilege

Contents

Contents

Acknowledgments

> A thief has only one thing in mind—he
> wants to steal, slaughter, and destroy.
> But I have come to give you everything
> in abundance, more than you expect—
> life in its fullness until you overflow!
>
> —John 10:10 (TPT)

I thank the Lord for allowing me to enlighten myself and all those who have the patience to read and study this book. All glory and thanks to our Lord Jesus Christ.

I also thank God for warrior notes through which the Lord Jesus enhanced my spiritual walk and helped me up the ladder of intimacy with Him. The Holy Spirit let me, and I became an online warrior-notes student in 2020 when I needed a place to fellowship. This drew me closer to the Lord Jesus. The prayers edified my spirit beyond measure, and the teachings helped to build my faith. This has been a crucial achievement in my spiritual growth.

Further thanks to Sid Rod. Romans 10:16 tells us, "So faith comes by hearing, and hearing by the word of God." Through Mr. Sid's *It's Supernatural* television show, my hunger to pursue spiritual realities increased and solidified my hope in the Lord Jesus to where I am today, wrapped in the love of the anointed one.

I also thank my family, especially my lovely mother, who has always supported me through good and challenging times. To God be all the glory!

Most people never understand that humanity is on a pilgrimage and will one day depart from this earth. The earthly suit (matter) that the soul and spirit envelope at conception is just a requirement to walk the earth as a man or a woman. This earth is a training ground where God sends His children to become evolved souls, to overcome obstacles, and to resist all forms of evil gratification that comes with the flesh.

Our pursuit, however, has been the acquisition of earthly wealth, which is not our ultimate purpose on earth. This shuts the soul and spirit, dims their lights, and propels us farther away from our goal.

Introduction

While in transit from Belgium to New York City, I had an open vision. An angel of the Lord sat next to me and explained that the United States is not how many people perceive it; life is not as easy as many think it is. It may seem that US citizens have everything, but at the same time, they have nothing. The angel concluded by telling me that when I got to the United States, I would witness things for myself.

After a few years in the United States, I graduated with an associate's degree in surgical technology. In the second year of pursuing a bachelor's degree in nursing, I had an open vision. The Lord told me to stop what I was doing and to do what He asked me to do. Before this, I'd had an open vision in which the Lord summoned me into ministry. I thought I would be a minister and a nurse, but the Lord wanted me to be fully committed to ministry.

As time went by, everything the angel told me became absolute truth. People own large houses and expensive cars but live in debt. These debts become a large cord around the neck, and everyday life is characterized by restless hard work to get the debt off their necks. Little time is set apart for the family or the education of children, which is the foremost responsibility of parents. Like drops of water eventually become an ocean, acquiring and saving material goods is the mindset of most immigrants who pursue wealth. They work hard to support the low-income families they left behind in third-world countries, with little or no time set apart for the spiritual building, which is the principal purpose of humans on earth. They follow the lifestyle they see and become birds of a feather. The soul is neglected, and the spiritual spark is gradually diminished until nothing is left but the earthly envelope that humans have on this physical journey.

We should always be mindful that, as spiritual beings, our souls are fed with light or darkness, just as our planet is made of day and night, depending on the activity in which we get involved. We also should be mindful that when our journeys on this earth come to an end and our fleshly envelopes are taken off, we will return to the presence of our heavenly Father and give Him an account of what we did with the gifts He invested in us.

The Lord Jesus wants us to pursue God's kingdom above all, which is the only way to avoid opening doors for darkness to creep into our souls. The practice of evil and satisfying the flesh has become the norm. This desire has crept deeply into the church, such that most leaders who are supposed to uplift the gospel of our Lord Jesus feel uncomfortable preaching the truth. Topics like fornication, adultery, and homosexuality become words too heavy for the tongue to utter. Very few intercessors supplicate for the salvation and gifts of the Holy Spirit.

After reading the revelations of our Lord Jesus Christ, as received through nineteenth-century Christian visionary Gottfried Mayerhofer, and their conformity to the Holy Scriptures, I concluded that they were authentic. Mayerhofer was born in Munich in 1807 to a notable German family. In 1870, at age sixty-three, Mayerhofer received the gift of hearing the inner word and accomplished this noble task for the Lord—as did Christian mystic and visionary Jakob Lorber—until his death in 1877.

Mayerhofer developed a cataract and had to undergo eye surgery. Afterward, he chose to dictate to a close friend the words the inner voice gave him. Through his efforts, several works originated. Many revelations relating to the creation, to life, to the road to salvation, communication with the spiritual world, and many other fundamental questions of life were presented.[1]

The Lord teaches us how to supplicate, as He mentioned in His sermon to Mayerhofer:

> I wanted to keep reminding them of their impotence, of how incapable they were of achieving things by themselves and wanted thus also to keep alive the memory of My activity and life in their midst, because only in this way—with spiritual aspirations—would they evaluate the things of this world correctly and not misinterpret them. This way of supplication was to bring about a constant growth of faith in Me, Who—although no longer visible—was still always with them spiritually. This helped them believe in My descent from above and pass on to others this unshakable faith in guidance by a supreme being as a Creator, Supporter, Lord, and Father. I, as God, did not require their supplications and had known in advance for eons of times what they needed and what was best for them. The sole purpose of supplication was to awaken in them and people in general, to have confidence in Me that I am not a God Whose greatness was to make the tiny human being tremble. But that I, a God and a Supreme Being, am accessible to My children and created beings as a loving Father through a meek approach, through ardent

---

[1] Triunity 54–55.

supplication or prayer which a loving Father can only grant, and not by a God who is a severe judge.[2]

The question is, how can the soul be nourished if only one of seven days a week is allocated for feeding the spirit and soul, which is achieved by spending time in God's presence? Instead, the soul is fed with gossip, perverted music and movies, hatred, fornication, adultery, theft, covetousness, lies, lust, and so forth for the remaining six days of the week.

I pray to God that this book will unveil the spiritual impact of the things in which we get involved, knowingly or unknowingly, as we turn the pages, by His grace.

---

[2] Gottfried Mayerhofer, "The Proper Supplication," Twenty-Fourth Sermon of Jesus (March 19, 1872).

Chapter 1

Man Blessed through Offspring

The creation of man occurred on the sixth day of God's creation. A human being is made of spirit, soul, and body. The spirit and soul always have been with God. The earthly envelope, which is the flesh, is formed in the womb at conception, except for the first man, Adam, and the first woman, Eve, whom God created as adults in their twenties before breathing souls into them.

Just as a meal is prepared and a table set for a guest, God, Creator of the entire universe, set the table before creating the first man. He created the earth and everything in it, such that man would have everything ready and set for him to enjoy the fullness thereof. All these material things that God set before man demonstrate the Father's goodness to His children. Above all these, only one blessing came forth from God's mouth to the man and woman He had created:

> And God blessed them, and God said unto them, be fruitful, and multiply, and replenish the earth, and subdue it: and have dominion over the fish of the sea, and over

the fowl of the air, and over every living thing that moveth upon the earth. (Genesis 1:28 KJV)

The first man, Adam, was blessed through his seed. Jesus defines a seed in His teachings, in the parable of the sower, as follows:

> Behold, infinity is contained within the seed. From a seed, there keep genuine products of the same kind to which the seed belongs. Thus, it was arranged at the creation of the material world that I created things only once individually. I included within them the germ for further reproduction so that the initial effect, the evolvement out of itself, would not cease in eternity as long as the elements in the soil and in the air needed for the development of the seed are available. As the seed of a tree carries within it all the nuclei for its future destination, thus My Word, which as a product of My Spirit keeps producing something new incessantly, never passes but continues forever. Therefore, John said: "In the beginning was the Word … and the Word was God!"[3]

God is eternal; so too are His words. Man's seed brings forth his children; thus, man cannot have dominion on earth without offspring. The strength of a nation depends on its population. If a man cannot propagate, given that he is mortal, there will be no way that humanity can continue to exist. According to the natural laws of God, for any beings to live on earth, they must put on earthly suits—the flesh made from the dust of the earth that clothes or envelopes humans' souls

---

[3] Gottfried Mayerhofer, "The Parable of the Sower," Eleventh Sermon of Jesus (January 20, 1872).

and spirits. The first covenant made between God and man was the blessing to procreate in the flesh:

> And I will make of thee a great nation, and I will bless thee, and make thy name great, and thou shalt be a blessing. (Genesis 12:2 KJV)

The greatness of Abraham's name was not just accomplished through the acquisition of tremendous material wealth among other men. God also referred to his generation through the continuation of his descendants and seed. With lots of material wealth, Abraham knew very well that all he had worked for and acquired would be in vain if he had no offspring to inherit it. This is the reason why he supplicated God about his childlessness:

> And Abram said, Lord GOD, what wilt thou give me, seeing I go childless, and the steward of my house is this Eliezer of Damascus? (Genesis 15:2 KJV)

Abraham knew well that no matter how many years man survived life, it would amount to nothing, given that man's journey on earth was temporal and must end one day, when the time allocated for his stay on earth was accomplished. If life ends and the soul is well trained, he or she will be considered worthy to return to the heavenly Father's kingdom as sons and daughters of God. But if returned with stains, it will be cast down to hell.

The blessings of children are another way to help humans in old age. When parents get old, their children and grandchildren provide help for their daily needs. Childbearing is a fundamental privilege granted to humans by God, allowing humans to participate in His creation. This starts with a family of two living together in harmony, which eventually grows and spreads to an entire population. This is how the book of Proverbs describes grandchildren:

> Children's children are the crown of old men, and the glory
> of children are their fathers. (Proverbs 17:6 KJV)

Our grandchildren are considered crowns of glory on our heads, symbols of power, honor, and status. The Lord blesses individuals with children, regardless of their weakness to take care of them, because God Himself is their caretaker and provider. Children help parents to become more responsible and less self-seeking, as life is no longer focused on self but on the well-being of the children. Also, children are joyous rewards from the union of a husband and wife. The Lord refers to them as the fruit of the womb:

> Lo, children are a heritage of the LORD: and the fruit of
> the womb is his reward. As arrows are in the hand of a
> mighty man, so are children of the youth. Happy is the
> man that hath his quiver full of them: they shall not be
> ashamed, but they shall speak with the enemies in the
> gate. (Psalm 127:3–5 KJV)

God emphasizes the blessing of those whose homes are filled with children, for they represent strength to defeat an enemy.

We are God's people, and therefore, the children are His. God uses our children to empower us and to help us overcome and accomplish much in life through them, especially in old age. Humanity should never forget that the children born are spirits sent by God through the womb, to put on the earthly suit and walk the earth through them. Humankind, through its pursuits, has opened doors for the evil one, who targets these God-ordained blessings and privileges by obstructing a journeyed soul from accomplishing his or her purpose.

The Enemies: Principalities and Demons

The battle of humans and their offspring against fallen angels and demons has always been the greatest challenge of humanity. God created everything to be perfect, and all functioned in heaven harmoniously until the fall of Lucifer and the host of angels under his command. This great angel, the light-bearer, was a pinnacle of perfection. His fall, along with the host of angels under his command, resulted from disobedience to God's command. When he was asked to bow to the first created man, Adam, he refused and responded:

> "But you said in your heart, 'I will ascend to heaven; I will raise my throne above the stars of God; I will sit on the mount of assembly in the remote parts of the north. I will ascend above the heights of the clouds; I will make myself like the Most High.' But in fact, you will be brought down to Sheol, to the remote recesses of the pit, the region of the dead." (Isaiah 14:13–14 AMP)

In the above scripture, Lucifer said "I" five times, which is the number of grace. It caused him to fall from grace, as the prophet Isaiah exclaimed,

> How you have fallen from heaven, O star of the morning [light-bringer], son of the dawn! You have been cut down to the ground, you who have weakened the nations [king of Babylon]! (Isaiah 14:12 AMP)

The rebellion of Lucifer and the hosts under his command triggered the eruption of a battle in heaven, which resulted in their exclusion. Revelation 12:7–8 explains:

Then a terrible war broke out in heaven. Michael and his angels fought against the great dragon. The dragon and his angels fought back. But the dragon did not have the power to win, and they could not regain their place in heaven. (TPT)

Lucifer and his hosts were cast off and lost their dwelling in the Shechinah of God's glory and became principalities and powers of the second heaven (Ephesians 6:12). Henceforth, enmity was established between humans and these principalities, who are bent on making sure that humans' souls and spirits should not return to God. These evil spirits blame humans for their fall.

As humans propagated and multiplied, with beautiful daughters birthed to them, sons of God took them as wives. The union of the immortal supernatural beings with mortal flesh resulted in strange flesh, and they bore giants—the Nephilim. This union corrupted the deoxyribonucleic acid, or DNA, of humans and rendered it irredeemable. These fallen beings brought humans all sorts of evil and witchcraft. Perversion and wickedness increased on the earth to a level that not only humans but all beasts and reptiles were corrupted.

Only Noah and his family were found undefiled before God, with uncompromised DNA. God grieved for having created humans on the earth and had to destroy all flesh with a flood, but He rescued Noah and his family with the ark He had commanded Noah to build (Genesis 6).

When Noah and his family and all the animals to be recused entered the ark, God shut the door behind them, and it rained for forty days and forty nights. Since every living thing is made of a body, spirit, and soul, only the flesh of the perverted humans, reptiles, and giant Nephilim and all else that was corrupted was destroyed in the flood, but not the spirits and souls. The souls were cast to hell, while the evil spirits roamed the earth restlessly as demons. Because nothing can function in the earthly realm without matter or flesh, these disembodied evil spirits have invaded or possessed humans' souls to operate through them.

The evil spirits are specific in their functions and characteristics. Many can possess a person at once.

> For Jesus had already said to the spirit, "Come out of the man, you evil spirit." Then Jesus demanded, "What is your name?" And he replied, "My name is Legion, because there are many of us inside this man." Then the evil spirits begged him again and again not to send them to some distant place. (Mark 5:8–10 NLT)

The demons asked the Lord Jesus not to send them to a distant place, fearing they would lose the territorial domain. These wicked humans, who once lived on earth but choose the devil's wicked ways, remain in his command as disembodied spirits.

> But when the Pharisees heard about the miracle, they said, "No wonder he can cast out demons. He gets his power from Satan, the prince of demons." (Matthew 12:24)

Unfortunately, many people continue to be deceived by material wealth and willingly open themselves to these principalities and demons. Others are possessed because they are trapped in the practice of evil pleasures. Some people are ignorant of the consequences of the things they do, which invites the spirits' presence and influence in their lives. These demonic spirits will stop at nothing to steal humans' blessings. Whatever method is used, the devil and his hordes will try to eliminate humans and their offspring.

Chapter 2

The Modern Method of Child Slaughter

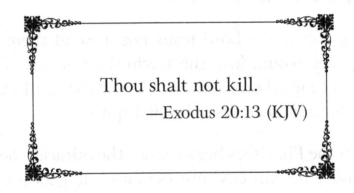

Thou shalt not kill.

—Exodus 20:13 (KJV)

Abortion

In 2019, I had a vision. In this vision, the Lord showed me that every human being is wired to Him spiritually. These connections to God are similar to a fetus being connected to the mother, through an umbilical cord. I saw these umbilical cords as made of bright lights, but their brightness varied, reflecting the person's lifestyle. If a person lives and walks uprightly before God, the cord and soul are bright, but if the person's life is defined by material gratifications and the person strays from God, the cord and soul are dim or darkened.

The following are the practices the devil beguiles humans to carry out that dim and darken the light of the cord and soul.

The ultimate method used by the devil to steal humans' greatest blessing is abortion. This is an unspeakable form of child slaughter, in the guise of the caressing term *abortion*—it just has to sound right in the ears to conceal such a horrible act of murder. Abortion is removing pregnancy tissue, products of conception, or the fetus and placenta from the uterus, or ending a pregnancy by removal or expulsion of an embryo or fetus. The human body is made of tissues, and the product of conception is a child.

There are two adapted modern methods of child slaughter. This atrocious act is performed either medically or surgically. Either method used to kill an unborn child does not eliminate the evil of its nature. The fact is that abortion is driven by a spirit of murder and has spiritual ramifications.

Medically, abortion pills are prescribed to block necessary hormones required for the survival, growth, and development of a pregnancy and to detach the fetus from the uterine wall. This is an outrageous form of fetus strangulation, achieved through starvation and squeezing. It causes contractions of the uterine wall and the cervix to open and expel the already-dead fetus. This is followed by a consequential effect of painful, intense cramps with heavy bleeding that may lead to death.

In a surgical abortion, the patient is sedated with anesthesia. A speculum is used to keep the vaginal walls apart, the cervix is dilated, and forceps are used to cut and dismantle the fetus into small pieces. These dismantled body parts of the fetus are suctioned from the uterus with other related pregnancy material.

Illegal abortion was common before it was officially legalized. The US Supreme Court ruling in Roe v. Wade in 1973 intends to protect women's right to choose to eliminate a pregnancy or to kill an unborn child without excessive restriction. When hidden evil creeps out of the dark, and a nation embraces it rather than condemns it, it signifies, spiritually, that demons have been given great authority to operate over that nation, at the expense of holy angels. Thus, evil prevails over good. Child conception is described by King David in the book of Psalms as follows:

> You formed my innermost being, shaping my delicate inside and my intricate outside, and wove them all together in my mother's womb. I thank you, God, for making me so mysteriously complex! Everything you do is marvelously breathtaking. It simply amazes me to think about it! How thoroughly you knew me, Lord! You even formed every bone in my body when you created me in the secret place, carefully, skillfully shaping me from nothing to something. You saw who you created me to be before I became me! Before I'd ever seen the light of day, the number of days you planned for me were already recorded in your book. (Psalm 139:13–16 TPT)

The above Bible verses unveil the invisible hand of God and the spiritual aspects of fetal growth and development. So the question is, what decision has a human on the life he or she cannot create nor tell how it is created? How can an individual be born of the womb, grow up, and quickly forget that he or she came from the same womb by eliminating others on the same path? Over 63 million children have been slaughtered since the legalization of abortion. This number is equivalent to the total population of the United Kingdom.

Those who recognize such a brutal war declared on the sanctity of life but give a blind eye and a deaf ear to it created room for it to become a God-forbidden norm in the nation. One may argue that it is just blood and tissue, and nothing is fully formed. Yes, it is blood, and when shed, a blood sacrifice and covenant is made with demons. For it is written:

> They sacrificed their sons and their daughters to the demons; they poured out innocent blood, the blood of their sons and daughters, whom they sacrificed to the idols of Canaan, and the land was polluted with blood. (Psalm 106:37–38 ESV)

Our lands are indeed polluted with the innocent blood of the unborn. An outcry swells because of the blood of innocent, unborn children, from the earth before the throne of God. God had assigned and sent those spirits to earth for His mission, just as every human being on this earth was sent by God for a mission. No one can deny that every heartbeat stopped through abortion, whatever the reason may be, is a compelling way to back the elimination of humanity, which is the great goal of the evil one to hinder God's plans and agenda on the earth through deceived human beings.

Abortionists, with their abortion clinics and surgical settings, use persuasive terms like *excellent procedure, safe abortion methods, convenient methods, expel the pregnancy, compassionate patient care, slightly, gently*—the list goes on. These terms cannot hide the invisible blood-drinking demons with long claws behind the veil of abortion that accompanies women after they make their bodies into evil altars.

> The Lord God said to the serpent, "Because you have done this, you are cursed more than all the cattle, And more than any animal of the field; On your belly, you shall go, And dust you shall eat All the days of your life." (Genesis 3:14 AMP)

It is also written, "The Lord God formed, that is, created the body of the man from the dust of the ground, and breathed into his nostrils the breath of life, and the man became a living being [an individual complete in body and spirit]" (Genesis 2:7 AMP). The physical material used to create humans—the food for the serpent or devil—is composed of one thing: dust of the earth.

People have been tremendously manipulated to believe that this absurd act of abortion is a solution that will resolve unprecedented problems, but they don't consider the spiritual detriment that the act of butchering of the unborn has on personal life and society. This atrocity is committed under the guise of fixing the problems of overpopulation, in some cases, or that one is not financially secure, or that pregnancy is a hindrance to achieving one's educational goal. Once these seeds of deception are sown in the human mind and conceived in the heart, individuals set out to destroy and eliminate their own offspring, something the beast of the wild cannot comprehend.

It is ridiculous to rely on any of the above-mentioned excuses for eliminating and preventing spirits from enveloping the earthly coat and rightfully walking the earth, through conception and development in the womb. A government should not allow abortion to resolve overpopulation, as some governments of the world do, as the book of Psalms reminds us:

> God claims the world as His. Everything and everyone belongs to Him! He's the one who pushed back oceans to let the dry ground appear, planting firm foundations for the earth. (Psalm 24:2–3 TPT)

In humans' tiny minds and common ways of reasoning, they want to convince themselves that God, the Father of all creation, is unaware of the proportion of space on the earth to the spirits that He, the

Creator, sent to this planet for their evolution and spiritual maturity. Blinded by greed, humans have forgotten that the earth is the garden of God, which He created for all humanity. And every soul must return to God at the end of his or her earthly course. And everyone will give an account to the Creator as to how they made use of the spiritual virtues invested in them.

Rape

According to the *Merriam-Webster Dictionary*, rape is unlawful sexual activity. Usually, sexual intercourse is carried out forcibly or under threat of injury against a person's will on a person younger than a certain age or one incapable of valid consent because of mental illness, mental deficiency, intoxication, unconsciousness, or deception.

Rape is the primary weapon of justification used by the devil for the advanced and legalized slaughter of the unborn. Regrettably, humans have fallen into this trap of the evil one by killing his blessings. The devil runs in a circle and uses evil methods to get an evil desire accomplished. It is unacceptable to respond to a victim who is tied down with demons of rape by opening oneself to blood-sucking evil spirits. The following is the heavenly principle that the Lord Jesus taught that is to be practiced if faced with such situations:

> "Your ancestors have also been taught, 'Take an eye in exchange for an eye and a tooth in exchange for a tooth.' However, I say to you, don't repay an evil act with another evil act. But whoever insults you by slapping you on the right cheek, turn the other to him as well. If someone is determined to sue you for your coat, give him the shirt off your back as a gift in return." (Matthew 5:38–42 TPT)

The Lord Jesus admonishes us in the above verse not to repay evil for evil. In a circumstance where rape ends in pregnancy, turn to God, the giver of all life, and say to Him, "Lord, this is the soul I received from you as a victim possessed by the spirit of rape, rapped me." If abortion is committed, a child is killed, the souls and the bodies of those involved in the act of abortion are defiled, and the devil celebrates his mission accomplished. Every child is from God, no matter what means the child came through. God told His prophet Jeremiah:

> Before I formed thee in the belly I knew thee, and before
> thou camest forth out of the womb I sanctified thee, and
> I ordained thee a prophet unto the nations. (Jeremiah
> 1:5 KJV)

The above verse says God knows every child before he or she is formed in the womb. For this reason, every pregnancy is to be openly embraced. Let God, the great rewarder of His children, significantly reward us for our troubles and for refusing to grant the desires of the evil one. We must choose good to prevail over evil. God promises in Isaiah, "Instead of shame and dishonor, you will enjoy a double share of honor. You will possess a double portion of prosperity in your land, and everlasting joy will be yours" (Isaiah 61:7 NLT).

God promised honor instead of shame and dishonor, which empowers us to take the next step required to move on from the abuse of rape. Thus, one finds a place within the heart to forgive the perpetrator and pray for his or her redemption. It is essential to forgive because unforgiveness is one of the great sins that darkens the soul and separates many from the kingdom of God. The Lord Jesus, while on the cross, prayed for the forgiveness of those who crucified Him (Matthew 24:23). Our pardon depends on our ability to pardon those who sin against us. Our Lord Jesus teaches the following about forgiveness:

> And when you pray, make sure you forgive the faults of others so that your father in heaven will also forgive you. But if you withhold forgiveness from others, your Father withholds forgiveness from you. (Matthew 6:14–15 TPT)

When the apostle Peter asked the Lord Jesus how many times he should forgive someone who sinned against him, Jesus told Peter to forgive not just seven times but seventy times seven times (Matthew 18:21–22). In this conversation, they did not specify a particular sin to be forgiven or its gravity. Forgiveness is the best way of telling God; "I surrender my situation in your hands." The Lord Jesus died on the cross and shed His blood for all of us. Let Him avenge us, as the apostle Paul wrote,

> Beloved, never avenge yourselves, but leave the way open for God's wrath and His judicial righteousness; for it is written in Scripture, "Vengeance is Mine, I will repay," says the Lord. (Romans 12:19 AMP)

Given that God has a reason for everything, let Him be placed ahead of every circumstance. A child may come into a person's life through rape, but God may decide to resolve much in the life of a victim of rape through that child. Tell the devil to his face that he will not accomplish his evil objective of murder through you.

Another unimaginable act against the unborn is the deliberate killing for the purpose of tissue extraction. The use of babies' tissues to manufacture vaccines is an ideology from the pit of hell, propagated by those who sit and dine with Satan himself. It could be put in better terms as a hungry mother who kills her baby and feed on the tissues.

This reveals the extent to which humans have opened themselves to blood-sucking demons. Oh, how wicked humans have become! The devil is playing the same old games, going around in circles. The evil one produces viruses, spreads them among people, and brainwashes people to kill their unborn children, in addition to the mystery diseases inflicted under the guise of producing vaccines.

Chapter 3

The Ancient Method of Child Slaughter

Every human being's soul and spirit on earth preexisted with God in the spirit realm from the foundation of the world before incarnating in the flesh. In ancient days, before advanced technology, the devil achieved this goal of child murder by selectively killing male children immediately after birth. Now, due to technological advancement, such horrors are committed in the womb before birth.

The devil used men in positions of high authority to kill male babies when he suspected that God intended to fulfill a promise or prophecy through a child and accomplish great goals. From the birth of the patriarch Abram to the birth of our Lord Jesus Christ, God incarnate, the devil made every attempt to stop their existence.

The Attempt to Slay Abram (Abraham)

The Lord God intended to create the world's nations through Abram, so He changed his name from Abram to Abraham, meaning "the father of all nations," indicating his destiny. In an attempt to obstruct God's purpose, the devil used Nimrod, a ruler, to kill all male children after birth. A detailed account of the birth of Abraham in *The Legends of the Jews* reads thus:

> Terah married Emtalai, the daughter of Carnabo, and the offspring of their union was Abram. His birth has been read in the stars by Nimrod, for this impious king was a cunning astrologer, and it manifest to him that a man will be born in his day who will rise up against him and triumphantly give the light to his religion. In his terror at the fate foretold him in the stars, he sent for his princes and governors and asked them to advise him in the matter. They answered and said unanimous advice is that "thou should build a great house, station guards at the entrance thereof and make known in the whole of thy realm that all pregnant women shall repair thither together with their midwives who are to remain with them why they are delivered. When the days of a woman to be delivered are fulfilled, and the child is born, it shall be the duty of the midwife to kill it if it is a boy, but if a child is a girl, it shall be kept alive, and the mother shall receive gifts, and costly garments and the herald shall be proclaimed. This is done unto the woman who bears a daughter." The king was pleased with this council, and he had a proclamation published through his whole kingdom summoning all the architects to build a great house for him sixty Ls high and eighty wides. After it was completed, he issued a second proclamation summoning all pregnant women hither there. They were to remain until their confinement officers were appointed to take the woman to the house, and guards were stationed in it and about it to prevent the woman

from escaping thence. He further sends midwives to the house and commanded them to slay the men's children at their mother's breasts. But if a woman bore a girl, she would be arrayed in business silk and embroidered garment and great honors. No less than seventy thousand children were slaughtered thus. Then angels appeared before God and spoke, "Seest thou not what he doth thou sinner and blasphemer Nimrod, son of Canary who slays so many innocent babes that have done no harm?" God answered and said, "Ye holy angels, I know it, and I see it for I neither slumber nor sleep. I behold, and I know the secret things and the things are revealed, and ye shall witness what I will do unto this sinner and blasphemer, for I will turn my hand against him to chastise him." It was about this time that Terah espoused the mother of Abraham, and she was with child, and when her body grew large at the end of three months of pregnancy, her countenance became pale. Terah said unto her, "What ails thee, my wife, that thy countenance is so pale and thou body is so swollen?" She answered and said, "Every year, I suffer from this malady." But Terah would not be put off thus. He insisted, "Show me thy body; it seems to me thou art big with child. If that be so, it behooves us not to violet the command of our god Nimrod." When he passed his hand over her body, there happened a miracle. The child rosed until it lay beneath her breast, and Terah can feel nothing with his hands. He said to his wife, "thou didst speak truly" and not become visible until the day of her delivery. When her time approached, she left the city in great terror and wandered towards the desert, walking along the edge of a valley until she happened to cross a cave. She entered this refuge, and the next day she was seized with throws, and she gave birth to a son.[4]

Abraham was a devout lover of God who exposed Nimrod's deceptive schemes, as he had declared himself a god and caused his subjects to worship him. The abortionists in our society today have replaced the kings and midwives that the devil used in the past to slaughter babies. Foreseeing that Abraham was to be the father of all nations, the devil had to kill seventy thousand children to prevent the birth of one child.

The Attempt to Slay Moses

The Israelites were enslaved by the Egyptians for four hundred years. God had promised to liberate His people, the Israelites, and it was to be done through His servant Moses. Conscious of this, the devil used Pharaoh, the ruler of Egypt, to kill thousands of male babies in an attempt to hinder God's plan of setting the Israelites free from bondage. The book of Exodus elucidates thus:

> Then the king of Egypt said to the Hebrew midwives, one of whom was named Shiphrah and the other Puah, "When you serve as midwife to the Hebrew women and see them on the birthstool, if it is a son, you shall kill him, but if it is a daughter, she shall live." But the midwives feared God and did not do as the king of Egypt commanded them but let the male children live. So, the king of Egypt called the midwives and said to them, "Why have you done this, and let the male children live? "The midwives said to Pharaoh, "Because the Hebrew women are not

---

[4] Louis Ginzberg, *The Legends of the Jews* (1953), vol. 1, chap. 5.

like the Egyptian women, for they are vigorous and give birth before the midwife comes to them." So, God dealt well with the midwives. And the people multiplied and grew very strong. And because the midwives feared God, he gave them families. Then Pharaoh commanded all his people, "Every son that is born to the Hebrews you shall cast into the Nile, but you shall let every daughter live. (Exodus 1:15–22 KJV)

The Lord had prophesied to Jacob (Israel) in years past that He would free the Israelites from the bondage of slavery in Egypt. When the time approached for God to use His vessel for the liberation, the devil played his old cards to kill the male children.

The Attempt to Slay Jesus the Christ

The great blessings of human salvation had to be accomplished through the incarnation of God the Most High in an earthly garment. This caught the devil by surprise, yet he made every attempt to slay Jesus. The Creator of the universe is bound by His own laws to put on flesh to live on earth. He had to become an offspring of His creation to walk the earth. This expresses what extraordinary blessings the children of humans are to them. The salvation of humanity can only be given by God, and He did so by pouring out Himself to His creation as the blessing of a child. A detailed recount of the Lord's birth is given in the Gospel of Matthew:

And when the second year had passed, magi came from the East to Jerusalem, brought great gifts and made strict inquiry of the Jews saying, "Where is the king who has been born to you? For we have seen His star in the east and have come to worship Him." And the word of this came to King Herod. And it so alarmed him that he called together the scribes and the Pharisees and the teachers of the people asking them where the prophets had foretold that Christ should be born? And they said in Bethlehem of Judah. For it is written:

Thou Bethlehem in the land of Judah art by no means the least among the princes of Judah for out of thee shall come forth a Leader who shall rule my people Israel.

Then King Herod summoned the magi to him and strictly inquire when the star appeared to them. Then send them to Bethlehem, he said, "Go and make a strict inquiry about the child and when ye have found Him, bring word again that I may come and worship Him also." While the magi were going on their way, there appeared to them the star, which as it were a guide to them. Going before them until they came to where the child was. And when the magi saw the star, they rejoiced with great joy, and going into the house, they saw the child Jesus sitting in his mother's lap. Then they opened their treasures and presented great gifts to the blessed Mary and joseph. And the child Himself they offered each of them a piece of gold, and likewise one gave gold, another frankincense, and the third myrrh. And when they were going to return to King Herod, they were warned by an angel in their sleep not to go back to Herod. And they returned to their country by another road.

And when Herod saw that he had been played sports of by the magi, his heart swelled with rage, and he searches through all the roads wishing to seize them and put them to death. But when he could not find them at all, he sent anew to Bethlehem in all its borders and slew all of their children whom he found of two years old and under according to the time that he had ascertained from the magi. Now the day before this was done, Joseph was warned in his sleep by the angel of the Lord who said to him, "Take Mary and the child and go into Egypt by way of the desert." Joseph went according to the saying of the angel. (Matthew 16–17)

From the above perspective, we observe that even the Lord Jesus Christ, Creator of all existence, had to escape to stay alive. The birth of our Lord Jesus Christ on earth brought not only the redemption of humanity but human awareness of his spiritual heritage and how people can train their souls in the flesh and return to God where they came from, through Christ our Lord.

The question of whether a child should live is not our place to determine. God alone is the Creator of all. He alone has a purpose for every soul created, and He alone determines if a heartbeat should exist. Many are misled by the devil to kill their children. One simple question to ask oneself is, "What if someone had had the choice of determining my existence and had chosen to abort me while I was in the womb?"

May people wake up from their slumbers! How many great talents and gifts invested in unborn children have been destroyed by human slaughter with forceps and destructive chemicals? Many of life's problems remain unresolved because the solutions to the problems, invested in unborn children, were stripped away by the wicked act of abortion. Human beings must fear God and abandon wickedness!

Chapter 4

How to Claim the Blessing

The moment you came in
the door and greeted me,
My baby danced inside
me with joy!

—Luke 1:44 (TPT)

Abraham was able to sense the killing of male babies in the spirit, which was taking place in the natural while he was in his mother's womb, around the period of his birth. For this reason, he did not want his father to notice his growth in the womb. It is written that when Terah passed his hand over his wife's body, a miracle happened. The child rose until he lay beneath her breast, and Terah could feel nothing with his hands. This consciousness in the womb was similar to a situation with John the Baptist. As Mary's greeting reached

Elizabeth's ears—Elizabeth was pregnant with John at the time—it had a direct effect on the baby in her womb, and he leaped with joy.

Given that babies are blessings from God, the manner with which we welcome them on their journey from the spirit realm to the physical realm is incredibly significant. Thus, giving is one thing, and receiving is another. To receive and rightfully embrace these blessings, we first must understand that life begins at conception. Second, when a woman is pregnant, she no longer is alone but shares her body with another spirit and soul. She must be mindful of what she listens to or watches, given that the unborn baby within can only communicate with the outside world through the mother. The portals of entry into our souls are the eyes and ears. What enters through them determines the mindset, what the heart conceives, and what comes out of the mouth. The apostle Paul wrote in his letter to the Romans, "So, letting your sinful nature control your mind leads to death. But letting the Spirit control your mind leads to life and peace" (Romans 8:6 NLT).

The human soul consists of the mind, the emotions, and the will. What enters the soul determines a person's behavior and what he or she believes and does. Therefore, it is pertinent in determining the outcome of the spirit and soul of the unborn child. Occupying oneself with praise and worship and meditating on the Word of God should be a daily routine. Reading, proclaiming, and declaring the Word of God will have a significant influence on the soul of the unborn child. Pray to God to fill the child with the fruits of the Holy Spirit, as it is written:

> But the Holy Spirit produces this kind of fruit in our lives: love, joy, peace, patience, kindness, goodness, faithfulness, gentleness, and self-control. There is no law against these things! (Galatians 5:22–23 NLT)

There is power in spoken words, for God created the world with His spoken words. If a pregnancy is unexpected, a simple prayer—such as, "Lord, grant me the grace to accept this blessing"—will suffice. God is always close and listens to His children. After the child's birth, continue to occupy the child with watching Christian cartoons, listening to an audio Bible and godly musical praise, and worshipping, as these shape the child's mind.

Unfortunately, the devil has infiltrated social media and many governments of the world. Through the majority of social media outlets, the evil one has prevailed to brainwash our children.

Also, evil has crawled into the world's governments and uses wicked leaders to pass and implement abominable laws that are destructive to human souls. Thus, one must be aware of how children entertain themselves, both on the internet and social media, even if it is a cartoon network intended for children.

Video games are perilous for children as well. Most characters in video games are demons. When children play such games regularly, the evil spirits capture their minds, and they become addicted to the games. The characters in these games are cartoons, but the spirits behind them are real. They hunt our children; this must be considered because the devil does not want to leave a stone unturned. If we realize that the children God gives us are for His glory, and we teach them His will, we will be rewarded abundantly with God's blessings. God requires us to consecrate ourselves and our children to Him by trusting and seeking Him in all we do.

> Trust in the Lord completely, and do not rely on your own opinions. With all your heart, rely on him to guide you, and he will lead you in every decision you make. Become intimate with him in whatever you do, and he will lead you wherever you go. (Proverbs 3:5–6 TPT)

Let me recount an event that demonstrates the impact that evil cartoon characters have on the minds of our children. God revealed this to me in a dream when I became a born-again Christian. I used to watch a certain animated children's television show with my child. This cartoon portrays a large family with different characters. One child in the family is a vampire; another has a friend whose parents are gay, and another is a lesbian.

I went to bed one night and had a dream. In the dream, the little vampire I watched in the cartoon with my child stood in front of me with folded hands. I cast it away several times in the name of Jesus, but it would not move. Then I woke from the dream.

God showed me, through this dream, how the things with which we entertain our eyes and ears affect our minds. Behind the scenes of social media are very evil intentions, engraved with tremendous darkness, aimed at manipulating our minds and the minds of our children. Based on political correctness, all moral and ethical values in a person are destroyed. When the soul is fed with these things, the soul darkens, and it causes a walk with God to feel like swimming upstream.

The Spiritual Role of Babies

The main thing we fail to understand is the spiritual influence that babies have in our lives. Every activity in which we get involved creates a spiritual atmosphere around us, be it holy or evil. Babies are champions at bringing the Holy Spirit into our surroundings. As spirit beings, babies retain and speak the spiritual language for a few weeks after birth, which commonly is known as babbling. As they adapt to life on earth, the heavenly language is gradually replaced by the earthly language. This is retrieved later in life when we renounce sin, accept Jesus Christ, and get born again through the Holy Spirit. This is written in the book of Psalms:

> You have built a stronghold by the songs of babies. Strength rises up with the chorus of singing children. This kind of praise has the power to shut Satan's mouth. Childlike worship will silence the madness of those who oppose you. (Psalm 8:2 TPT)

The heavenly language uttered is pure, spiritual warfare, perfectly forged by the tongues of children, whose innocence gives no room for the accusing voice of the enemy. Our babies are literally prayer warriors and worshippers who fight our spiritual battles and stand in the gap for us. The apostle Paul says the following about the spiritual language in his epistle to the Romans:

> And in a similar way, the Holy Spirit takes hold of us in our human frailty to empower us in our weakness. For example, at times, we don't even know how to pray or know the best things to ask for. But the Holy Spirit rises up within us to super-intercede on our behalf, pleading to God with emotional sighs too deep for words. (Romans 8:26 TPT)

It is too deep for words; the mind cannot understand the things of the spirit. Babies do not know the mysteries they utter, and it's the same with a born-again Christian, except the Christian has the gift of the interpretation of spiritual language.

The enemy may make a person look at an unwanted pregnancy as an obstacle in the middle of more important life events, like school. The person also may feel unprepared or have other deficiencies, like insufficient finances or other fake excuses. God allows a pregnancy to occur as He foresees a future situation that will be resolved by the conceived child, with the gifts He invests in him or her.

Marriage is required for a man and a woman to start a family. This facilitates a child's upbringing by both parents and his or her proper education. If a woman conceives before she and the father of the conceived child are united, the child nevertheless should be brought forth. In that case, a conception is not "fixed" by committing an atrocity on the unborn child and the woman's body, for two wrongs do not make a right. We accept the baby and receive the blessing from God, and we let Him take care of the child He has sent through us.

As Jesus admonished us in the book of Matthew:

> "This is why I tell you to never be worried about your life, for all that you need will be provided, such as food, water, clothing—everything your body needs. Isn't there more to your life than a meal? Isn't your body more than clothing? Consider the birds—do you think they worry about their existence? They don't plant or reap or store up food, yet your heavenly father provides them each with food. Aren't you much more valuable to your father than they? So, which one of you by worrying could add anything to your life? And why would you worry about your clothing? Look at all the beautiful flowers of the field. They don't work or toil, and yet not even Solomon in all his splendor was robed in beauty like one of these! So, if God has clothed the meadow with hay, which is here for such a short time and then dried up and burned, won't he provide for you the clothes you need—you of little faith? So then, forsake your worries! Why would you say, 'What will we eat?' or 'What will we drink?' or 'What will we wear? For that is what the unbelievers chase after. Doesn't

your heavenly father already know the things your bodies require? So above all, constantly seek God's kingdom and his righteousness, then all these less important things will be given to you abundantly. Refuse to worry about tomorrow, but deal with each challenge that comes your way, one day at a time. Tomorrow will take care of itself." (Matthew 6:25–34 TPT)

God, the giver of all things, must be trusted and allowed to have His way in all matters of our lives, for He holds the future. He promised us in Psalm 139 that if we rise on the wings of the dawn, if we settle on the far side of the sea, even there, His hand will guide us. His right hand will hold us fast.

Chapter 5

Spiritual Implications of Abortion

The spiritual effects of abortion are more grievous than one could ever imagine, both on the aborted child and on the person involved in the act. This is because it transforms what is holy unto God and makes it a habitat of demon spirits. Abortion is the continuation of child blood sacrifice, made by offering children to an idol in the primordial days. According to the Old Testament, this act was performed by idol worshipers of Baal, Asherah, and Molech. The children are sacrificed to demons in the mother's womb before birth. The devil intends to counterfeit the Word of our Lord Jesus under the new covenant to worship God in spirit and truth.

Altars

Under the Old Testament, people gathered in specific locations—mountains, hills, plains, or valleys—for worship, where altars were erected to offer blood sacrifices.

> Then Abram removed his tent, and came and dwelt in the plain of Mamre, which is in Hebron, and built there an altar unto the LORD. (Genesis 13:81 KJV)

Sacrifices were offered to God from the erected altar. Any location where an altar is erected denotes a place of encounter between the spirit realm and the natural realm—where humans meet with God and holy angels or where humans meet with fallen angels and demonic spirits. This form of worship continued until Moses built the ark of covenant, as God required of him.

> They shall make an ark of acacia wood two and a half cubits long, one and a half cubits wide, and one and a half cubits high. You shall overlay the ark with pure gold, overlay it inside and out, and you shall make a gold border (frame) around its top. You shall cast four gold rings for it and attach them to the four feet, two rings on either side. You shall make [carrying] poles of acacia wood and overlay them with gold, and put the poles through the rings on the sides of the ark, by which to carry it. The poles shall remain in the rings of the ark; they shall not be removed from it [so that the ark itself need not be touched]. You shall put into the Ark the Testimony (Ten Commandments) which I will give you. (Exodus 25:10–17 AMP)

The Israelites carried the ark of God's covenant around the desert during the forty years they wandered in the wilderness. It was kept in tents when they camped. There, God's priests served Him and the Israelites before King Solomon built the temple where the ark was kept.

Despite the presence of God among the Israelites and the communications through His ark, many still bowed to idols. Idol worshipers erected altars. The children of those who bowed to these images became victims and were offered as food to the demonic spirits of Baal, Asherah, and Molech. This is related in Jeremiah as follows:

> They set up their abominations in the house that is called by my name to defile it. They built the high places of Baal in the Valley of the Son of Hinnom to offer up their sons and daughters to Molech, though I did not command them, nor did it enter into my mind, that they should do this abomination, to cause Judah to sin. (Jeremiah 32:34–35 ESV)

Under the New Testament, however, the Lord Jesus had a conversation with a Samaritan woman at the well, after sending His disciples to a nearby town to buy some food.

> The woman changed the subject. "You must be a prophet! So, tell me this: Why do our fathers worship God on this nearby mountain, but your people teach that Jerusalem is the place where we must worship. Who is right?" Jesus responded, "Believe me, dear woman, the time has come when you will worship the Father neither on a mountain nor in Jerusalem, but in your heart. Your people don't really know the one they worship, but we Jews worship out of our experience, for it's from the Jews that salvation is available. From now on, worshiping the father will not be a matter of the right place but with the right heart. For God is a Spirit, and he longs to have sincere worshipers

who adore him in the realm of the spirit and in truth."
(John 4:19–24 TPT)

In the above verses, the Lord reminds us that God is spirit and must be worshipped in spirit and truth. What brings God's presence is the state of a person's heart who comes into His presence, not the hills, mountains, physical structures, or buildings erected by people. The Lord Jesus emphasized, with regard to living temples (our bodies), it results that the devil, master of all counterfeits, eliminates the erected altars and requires a blood sacrifice, based on its spiritual significance. Demons show up for blood sacrifices made at any setting, as long as the act defiles the body and goes against the commandments of God.

Abortion clinics established in every corner of our society today replace the altars of Baal, Asherah, and Molech. Given that whatever an individual practices creates a specific atmosphere around him or her, either good or evil, the act of prayers and worship performed in spirit and truth opens up heavenly portals and brings forth the presence of God. Likewise, when an abortion is performed on individuals, their bodies are defiled, and evil portals are opened for demons to creep into their bodies or lives and feed on the blood. Thus, what is supposed to be a temple for an indwelling of the Holy Spirit becomes filth for demons.

As the apostle Paul says,

> Have you forgotten that your body is now the sacred temple of the Spirit of Holiness, who lives in you? You don't belong to yourself any longer, for the gift of God, the Holy Spirit, lives inside your sanctuary. You were God's expensive purchase, paid for with tears of blood, so by all means, then, use your body to bring glory to God. (1 Corinthians 6:19–20 TPT)

Given that our bodies are temples, they must be occupied by either holy or evil spirits. The evil spirits impact our lives in so many ways. First, the bloodshed through abortion is a blood covenant made with demon spirits. They are blood-sucking demons, commonly known as murder spirits. The spirits of murder that enhance abortion give access to spirit husbands and wives. A person who has had an abortion will find it difficult to get married or stay married because the main objective of these spirits is to hinder marriage. Very few people get married and maintain their homes with these hordes in their lives. If a person has committed abortion and does not become a born-again Christian, these spirits will continue to influence and torment the person's life. If the person remains single, there is a greater possibility that she will continue to prostitute herself and commit more abortions. The only way to overcome is through the power in the blood of Christ and the Holy Spirit. The apostle wrote,

> Don't you realize that together you have become God's inner sanctuary and that the Spirit of God makes his permanent home in you? Now, if someone desecrates God's inner sanctuary, God will desecrate him, for God's inner sanctuary is holy, and that is exactly who you are. (1 Corinthians 3:16–17 TPT)

The Holy Spirit is the light of God in the body and the body should always be kept holy. Abortion stains the soul and allows these spirits to destroy the body and to deposit all sorts of diseases, and the person runs the risk of the abortion rendering her barren.

Another unfortunate spiritual effect of abortion is that it gives authority to the spirit of death to take lives prematurely, irrespective of age or race. In Genesis, we read, "And the Lord said, 'What have you done? The voice of your brother's blood is crying to me from the ground'" (Genesis 4:10 ESV).

The blood of unborn children is innocent because they have never spoken a word or pointed a finger at someone to accuse the person. When the voices of the unborn children cry out to the Lord, complaining that they have been killed for no reason, this justifies the spirit of death.

The most vulnerable life, which is supposed to be protected, is not secured but eliminated. For instance, one may argue it is an individual's decision to abort or not to abort. Suppose a person who stands for abortion commits abortion and another person who does not stand for abortion never commits one. In this case, both individuals will suffer the consequences of such a deplorable act, committed by the one who stands for abortion.

As mentioned above, abortion gives legal authority for the spirit of death to take away lives prematurely, regardless of age or race. It does not matter if the person's purpose on earth is accomplished or not. It is the primary responsibility of all humanity to protect and defend the defenseless and most vulnerable. This is the reason why the Lord admonishes us, "You shall not give any of your children to offer them to Molech, and so profane the name of your God: I am the Lord" (Leviticus 18:21 ESV).

Thus, the voices of babes that were supposed to bring blessings into our families and homes through songs of worship and spiritual tongues are not there. Instead, our bodies are not only defiled, but the innocents' drops of blood point against those who failed to protect and defend them. We are God's creatures, created for His glory. We do not have any authority to determine if another person should exist.

The consequences of abortion are severe. The Lord Jesus warns that if anyone abuses a little one, it would be better for that person to have a heavy boulder tied around his or her neck and to be hurled into the deepest sea than to face the punishment he or she deserves for such an act (Matthew 18:6). This is why the Lord Jesus also reminds us of our inability to make one hair white or black (Matthew 5:36). In his letter to the Romans, the apostle Paul writes, "I appeal to you, therefore, brothers, by the mercies of God, to present your bodies as a living sacrifice, holy and acceptable to God, which is your spiritual worship" (Romans 12:1 ESV).

The verse above tells us that a holy lifestyle is a form of spiritual worship. Therefore, if the persons to whom God has given dominion over all creation on earth continues to gaze away from his or her Creator and offers up himself or herself as a vessel for evil spirits, there shall be no harmony on the earth, which is only brought about by love. God is love. Most men in positions of power, with straight ties around their necks, fight hard to support the course of abortion under the guise of human rights. A few of these men—with no wombs and without knowing how it feels to have a womb—may ignorantly fight for what they sincerely believe are human rights, without knowing the disastrous effects that such horrific acts have on humanity and society, but most of these men know absolutely what they are doing, and they represent those our Lord Jesus described when He said,

> You are the offspring of your father, the devil, and you serve your father very well, passionately carrying out his desires. He's been a murderer right from the start! He never stood with the truth, for he's full of nothing but lies—lying is his native tongue. He is a master of deception and the father of lies! (John 8:44 TPT)

Yes, the sons of their father, the devil, are rebellious and have rejected the love and truth of God, who know precisely what they are out for; that is, fighting and defending the supply of blood—food—for their father, the devil. Women must be wise and protect their bodies, for they are inner sanctuaries of the Holy Spirit. Anything that individuals call legal but is contrary to the laws and commandments of God must be shredded or flushed down the drain.

Chapter 6

Switching Off the Light of the Soul

The light of Christ brightens the human soul and empowers the spirit if we live in obedience to His Word and commandments. If we choose to shut our eyes and ears from the Word of God, which is truth, life, and light, then the journey on earth is futile. The sole purpose of earthly navigation is for spiritual growth and maturity and to return to God Almighty. He did not send His children to pursue fleshy gratifications and become unworthy of His glory. Paul wrote to the Corinthians:

> Surely, you must know that people who practice evil cannot possess God's kingdom realm. Stop being deceived! People who continue to engage in sexual immorality, idolatry, adultery, sexual perversion, homosexuality, fraud, greed, drunkenness, verbal, abuse or extortion—these will not inherit God's kingdom realm. (1 Corinthians 6:9–10 TPT)

Although abortion is the primary outrageous sin committed against humanity and the temple of the Holy Spirit, which turns off the light of the soul, other sins committed against the bodily temple, with similar detrimental effects, include homosexuality, adultery, and fornication.

Homosexuality

Homosexuality is when a person is sexually attracted to the same gender. This abominable practice is a perverted way of life, enhanced from the pit of hell and aimed at profaning the sanctity of marriage that was instituted by God Himself from the foundation of the world.

In May 2019, after worship and prayer, I waited on the Lord, and the Lord spoke to me, saying, "Do not feed on the love that does not swell with purity. The nakedness of Adam and Eve in the garden of Eden implied that all about them was pure before My eyes. It is the same with one who steps in the Holy of Holies—purity of heart. One has to be pure in My holy presence, without anything to hide. Adam and Eve had become one by knowing each other in union. So does My bride become one with Me and in Me."

The Lord was elucidating John 15 to me. God can only be part of a union that is established on the purity of His principles. He will reject a union in which the body is offered up to sin as instruments of wickedness, rather than to God or in conformity to His commandments.

Homosexuality is a significant way that the devil stops the propagation of humanity and destroys the souls of the individuals involved. Satan gets into the lives of victims who are trapped in desecrated homosexual lifestyles through broken and dysfunctional homes, rape, pornography, and molestations by family members, friends, or strangers. Also, verbal abuse, physical abuse, sexual abuse, emotional abuse, mental abuse, and pressure from peer groups are other methods that provide an open door for the devil to torment the minds of victims and cause them to question their sexual orientation, creating false feelings that are contrary to what God created them to experience.

It is absurd that many follow these false feelings, which fluctuate because they were not created that way. It is the same as feeling happy this week and sad the subsequent week, depending on the state of mind. The soul is made up of the mind, the will, and the emotions, which are commonly exposed to evil sexual spirits. The more these spirits are entertained, the more depraved the mind becomes.

The letter from the apostle Paul to the Romans admonishes us on spiritual growth and maturity:

> I've used the familiar terms of a "servant" and a "master" to compensate for your weakness to understand. For just as you surrendered your bodies and souls to impurity and lawlessness, which only brought more lawlessness into your lives, so now surrender yourselves as servants of righteousness, which brings you deeper into true holiness. For when you were bound as servants to sin, you lived your lives free from any obligation to righteousness.
>
> So tell me, what benefit ensued from doing those things that you're now ashamed of? It left you with nothing but a legacy of shame and death. But now, as God's loving servants, you live in joyous freedom from the power of sin. So consider the benefits you now enjoy—you are brought deeper into the experience of true holiness that ends with eternal life! For sin's meager wages is death, but God's lavish gift is life eternal, found in your union with our Lord Jesus, the Anointed One. (Romans 6:19–23 AMP)

One must be conscious of the invisible, controlling forces around us. We must be either slaves of righteousness or slaves of sin. Yet there is no slavery in doing righteous deeds, for they blossom into eternal life. But sinful deeds lead to death.

Thus, the lives of those involved in homosexuality are defined by anxiety, depression, addictions, and nervousness. They have to depend on medications to get through this challenging lifestyle, which results in addiction and, in many cases, suicide because demon spirits of gender confusion and homosexuality have imprisoned the victims' souls. As such, a spiritual battle goes on within the individuals' souls to set them free from the captivity and oppression of these evil spirits.

Concerning a marriage union. Jesus says,

> Such a union should be founded on true spiritual and moral love, the basis for a family life with mutual respect. Through My established natural law, the Law of Pairing, I proposed the living together of two individuals. I wanted fruits to be propagated out of such love, which propagated and ennoble the better mental qualities of the one and the other. Thus, the Marriage Law, which I implanted in nature as an urge for propagation, was the cause for an everlasting gamut from being to being right up to Me. That was what I wanted, and what have you people made of it? A market with human flesh and the selling of souls.[5]

We learn in Genesis that God took one being from another in the creation of the first human beings. When God decided to create a mate for Adam, He separated part of him to form Eve so that when they united in marriage, they would become one heart and one mind, making their union harmonious. It was purposely for reproduction

---

[5] Gottfried Mayerhofer, "The Wedding in Cana," Eighth Sermon of Jesus (January 20, 1872).

that God separated Adam to make a woman from him. The book of Genesis says,

> So, the Lord God caused a deep sleep to fall upon the man, and while he slept, He took one of his ribs and closed up its place with flesh. And the rib that the Lord God had taken from the man he made into a woman and brought her to the man. Then the man said, "This, at last, is bone of my bones and flesh of my flesh; she shall be called woman because she was taken out of Man." (Genesis 2:21–23 ESV)

The Lord Jesus began His ministry at a wedding feast, the marriage of two people of the opposite sex. This illustrates the significance of marriage—it is not only for humans but for God's own union with His church. The devil is determined to disrupt humanity and return humans to the perverted days of Sodom and Gomorrah. Homosexuality is a filthy lifestyle practiced mainly by the afflicted. Such practices not only lessen man, created in God's image, to filth but make him a destructive soul and prevent him from attaining spiritual growth and maturity.

This is also an effective means of demonic seed harvesting. The seed of man, which is supposed to be his offspring, is offered up to demons and evil spirits. This impenitent sin is recounted in Genesis as follows:

> But before they lay down, the men of the city, the men of Sodom, both young and old, all the people to the last man, surrounded the house. And they called to Lot, "Where are the men who came to you tonight? Bring them out to us, that we may know them." Lot went out to the men at the entrance, shut the door after him, and said, "I beg you,

my brothers, do not act so wickedly. Behold, I have two daughters who have not known any man. Let me bring them out to you and do with them as you please. Only do nothing to these men, for they have come under the shelter of my roof." But they said, "Stand back!" And they said, "This fellow came to sojourn, and he has become the judge! Now we will deal worse with you than with them." Then they pressed hard against the man Lot and drew near to break the door down. (Genesis 19:4–9 ESV)

Evil spirits are wicked, and anything driven by them accomplishes wicked desires. God created everything with the light; it received life, and, in love, it can never be annihilated (John 1:4). When people stray too far from the laws of God, the light of God in them is extremely dimmed, and the moral aspects of life gradually depart from them. The greater the influence of demonic spirits in one's life, the darker the soul. This results in violence, wickedness, lust, and lack of self-control. A perverted individual is worse than the beast of the wild. This is because God gave people free will to either obey His words and take on the image of God or disobey them and become less than the beast of the wild, over which people are supposed to have dominion.

Homosexual sin is the reason why God had to destroy the twin cities of Sodom and Gomorrah. When the evil one leads people to practice such perverse acts, it affords him the right to rip away the warmth of love; their hearts become cold, and they feel rejected. The devil can always use the propaganda that this is love and that every person has the free will to express his or her love in whatever ways he or she sees fit. This is a lie from the father of all lies, intended to keep the doors open for him to come in and steal. Individuals should be mindful of how special they are to the Creator and be concious of the treasures invested in them, such that twins from the same womb do not have the same fingerprints.

In the same way, the gifts that God invests in every human are specific. The continuation of God's gifts in humans can be harvested only as they spread through offspring and become blessings to others. This cannot be achieved by a homosexual because seeds are not propagated but are sown to demons. If a man chooses not to bring forth seeds, it should only be to dedicate his life to the glory of God. That is, he does so because he is called by God, and his time is dedicated to God's services.

Homosexuality is driven by lust, not by love. A soul mate can only be someone of the opposite sex, ordained by God from the very creation of the first man and woman; that is, a joining back together of what was separated at the beginning of creation, to be united again as one. This recounts the reason why God had to destroy the twin cities that were filled with such filth:

> Then the Lord rained on Sodom and Gomorrah sulfur and fire from the Lord out of heaven. And he overthrew those cities, and all the valley, and all the inhabitants of the cities, and what grew on the ground. But Lot's wife, behind him, looked back, and she became a pillar of salt. (Genesis 19:24–26 ESV)

Everyone that wavers in righteousness remains a victim of sin. Jesus requires us to hold the plow and never look back, no matter the schemes that Satan uses to distract us. That is what Lot's wife failed to do—a sign of regret for the life she left behind. Homosexuality causes individuals to lose their personalities and dignity, stray from spiritual maturity, and forget in whose image they are created. They must get out of this outrageous lifestyle and never look back to it, no matter how the devil reminds them of their unworthiness. The most convincing argument is that everyone has the right and free will to live life as he or she sees fit. However, as it is written in Paul's letter to the Corinthians:

> It's true that our freedom allows us to do anything, but that doesn't mean that everything we do is good for us. I'm free to do as I choose, but I choose to never be enslaved to anything. Some have said, "I eat to live, and I live to eat!" But God will do away with it all. The body was not created for illicit sex, but to serve and worship our Lord Jesus, who can fill the body with himself. (1 Corinthians 6:12–13 TPT)

Human beings are conferred a free will to make the right choices and do the right things. In unions between a man and a woman, the man provides the seed, and the woman provides the fertile soil. If the seed is not released in the soil but is released elsewhere, it will be harvested by demonic spirits, and nothing is produced for the glory of God. These wicked spirits possess the people involved in such immoral practices and intensify their influence on them so that the people will keep up with the supply of seeds.

We see that God punished Onan and his brother, sons of Judah, for wasting their seeds:

> And Judah took a wife for Er, his firstborn, and her name was Tamar. But Er, Judah's firstborn, was wicked in the sight of the Lord, and the Lord put him to death. Then Judah said to Onan, "Go into your brother's wife and perform the duty of a brother-in-law to her and raise up offspring for your brother." But Onan knew that the

offspring would not be his. So, whenever he went into his brother's wife, he would waste the semen on the ground so as not to give offspring to his brother. And what he did was wicked in the sight of the Lord, and he put him to death also. (Genesis 38:6–10 ESV)

A typical modern method of seed wasting and seed harvesting is the use of condoms and masturbation. It is appalling that some medical practitioners advise their patients to practice such onanism and prescribe the use of condoms as the way of preventing sexually transmitted diseases, enhancing seed wasting.

Most scientists make every effort to uproot God and spirituality in all aspects of science. Every possible attempt is made to flush God down the drain. The question is, how will science prevail if the Master of all science is not at its center? These medical practitioners fail to enlighten the patients, who look to them for health solutions, of the dangerous impact of open portals that invite demons of seed harvesting and spirit husbands and wives into their lives because of such practices. It is imperative to spend time in the Word of God and be aware of deeds that are destructive to the soul.

Clean Case, Dirty Case

> Bless the Lord, O my soul, and all that is within
> me, bless his holy name! Bless the Lord, O my
> soul, and forget not all his benefits.
>
> —Psalm 103:1–2 (ESV)

The human body is made up of eleven distinct systems. These systems differ in biological functions, and God placed them at different levels in a spiritual hierarchy. All these systems and organs praise and worship God distinctly.

I had a vision in which the Lord Jesus stood before me like a mighty mountain. He needed all my attention, but behind me stood a blasphemer or a boaster not in the Lord. This blasphemer made all sorts of noise and distracted me from paying attention to the Lord. Every time I turned my head to look at this blasphemer, the Lord stretched out His hand, placed it on my jaw, and turned my face back toward His, that I might gaze into His eyes. But the noise from this blasphemer would not allow me to focus on the Lord. The Lord Jesus lifted His finger to the air and flung the blasphemer into a nearby lake. This blasphemer was drowning and unable to swim out of the lake.

I did not hear the noise again, which allowed me to focus my attention on the Lord and gaze deeply into His eyes without distraction. I could pay attention and capture what He intended to communicate in my mind. As soon as I understood what He was communicating to me, He suddenly transformed from a mighty mountain before me to a friendly man walking next to me. As I walked along with the Lord Jesus, my body parts individually recognized and praised Him. My eyes, ears, hair, and all parts of my body were praising Him uniquely, like what King David proclaimed in Psalm 103:1–2 (above).

The reproductive system and the digestive system comprise two of the eleven systems—the reproductive system for propagation and the digestive system to digest and absorb food. Suppose the organs of these two systems were compromised and had to be surgically operated on simultaneously. In this case, the reproductive organs would be classified as a "clean case" and be prioritized, while the digestive organs would be classified as a "dirty case" and surgery performed last. The instruments used to operate on the reproductive organs can be used on the digestive organs, but the instruments used to operate on the digestive organs cannot be used on the reproductive organs. This emphasizes the superiority of the reproductive organs over the digestive organs.

God has ordained the continuation of the human race through the reproductive organs, while the digestive organs are used to break food that is later excreted. The reproductive system is elevated on the ladder of the spiritual hierarchy to a higher level, as compared to the digestive system. Food is not the only source of survival. As the Lord Jesus quoted from the book of Deuteronomy during His temptation, "Man shall not live on bread alone, but on every word that comes from the mouth of God" (Matthew 4:4 NIV). Homosexuality disrupts the levels of hierarchy, as the apostle Jude writes in his epistle:

> In a similar way, the cities of Sodom and Gomorrah and nearby towns gave themselves to sexual immorality and the unnatural desire of different flesh. Now they all serve as examples of those who experience the punishment of eternal fire. (Jude 1:7 TPT)

In the above Bible verse, the apostle Jude mentions the words *different flesh*. The reproductive and digestive systems are different in function and cell specificity, with different levels of spiritual hierarchies that are not to join together. One of our Lord Jesus's main accomplishments during His earthly ministry was the healing of the sick. Since the devil's objective is to do the opposite of what God does, homosexuality is one of the tools used by this serpent of old to infect and spread diseases that make life miserable. When different body organs and systems join that are not supposed to, the flesh becomes strange, obstructing the proper functions of these organs and resulting in many contaminations and diseases; health is ultimately compromised. Our bodies, like the body of Christ, should not be given any room for evil desires. The devil will use the least-compromised body organ to penetrate and destroy the entire body.

> Boasting over your tolerance of sin is inappropriate. Don't you understand that even a small compromise with sin permeates the entire fellowship, just as a little leaven permeates a batch of dough? To remove every trace of your "leaven" of compromise with sin so that you might become new and pure again. For indeed, you are clean because Christ, our Passover Lamb, has been sacrificed for us. So now we can celebrate our continual feast, not with the old "leaven," the yeast of wickedness or bitterness, but we will feast on the freshly baked bread of innocence and holiness. (1 Corinthians 5:6–7 TPT)

Disruption of a single organ affects the entire body. If the devil intends to destroy the church of Christ, a common way to achieve his objective is to get in a prominent member of the church, through whom the entire church will be compromised. This same method is used in our bodies by getting through individual body organs to destroy the entire body. The apostle Paul also admonishes us in his letter to the Romans:

> Do not let any part of your body become an instrument of evil to serve sin. Instead, give yourselves completely to God, for you were dead, but now you have new life. So, use your whole body as an instrument to do what is right for the glory of God. (Romans 6:13 NLT)

A dangerous spirit in this age is political correctness, also erected on the shoulders of the deep church—those who say "Lord, Lord" but shall not enter the kingdom of God, for the Lord will indeed tell them on that day, "I never knew you." As evil creeps into the church, a few individuals will be hidden under the veil of political correctness to compromise the gospel's truth. They are bent on making sure that victims of homosexuality remained bound in the chains of this profane lifestyle. They work tirelessly, making sure that legislations are passed that ban counseling that could lead people out of this lifestyle. Family members and friends of these sufferers must stand firm and help them take back the sanity of their minds, emotions, and lifestyle from those who are determined to ruin them. The Lord says in Psalm 50:15, "And call upon me in the day of trouble; I will deliver you, and you shall glorify me" (ESV).

We have to turn to God for deliverance, for a person's identity is defined by his or her gender at birth. This definition is rooted in the soul. I studied the significant differences between the male and female genders in anatomical body structure and physiological body function in biology. A person's sex relates to its biological functions. For example, male and female genitalia, both internal and external, are different. Similarly, the levels and types of hormones present in male and female bodies are different.

Genetically, women have forty-six chromosomes, including two X chromosomes, denoted as XX, whereas men have forty-six, including an X and a Y chromosome, denoted as XY. The Y chromosome is dominant and carries the signal for the embryo to begin growing testes. These differences can not be altered by any physical transformation; they are rooted deep in the souls and spirits. The devil deceives most of his victims to change their sexuality and become transgender by undergoing several plastic surgery procedures, in which body organs are removed and replaced, with the intent to alter creation and look different. Also, hormones are injected and infused into the bodies to achieve female or male features. This serpent of old, the destroyer of human souls, does not disclose to his victims that God created man with a spirit, soul, and body. Our earthly garments—our bodies—that cover the spirit and soul can be altered at any time, just like a dress that is worn and taken off. But the soul and spirit are unchangeable. The effort to have a different outward look from who a person naturally is creates a significant conflict between the outer garment and the spirit and soul, disrupting the harmony of the spirit, soul, and body, making life miserable. The physical change did not result in a physiological and spiritual change, which causes one to struggle to walk and behave differently from who God created.

The gastrointestinal system, which houses about 70 percent of the immune system, is greatly abused by homosexuality. Also, about 90 percent of the human body is made up of water, with a large portion absorbed in the gut. When the large blood vessels lining the intestinal wall are compromised in homosexual acts, the normal safety process of fluid absorption is broken, leading to the common disease known as leaky gut, which triggers a ripple effect of autoimmune diseases.

Unfortunately, the devil has succeeded in blinding the eyes of many people and has beguiled them to submit to and support such imprisonment. Attempts made to free fellow humans from such traps have been characterized as hate speech. Those who sold their souls to that dragon of old, the devil, pretentiously discriminate, spread hate speech, and undermine minorities, including the use of all sorts of deceptive words that sound good to the ears but are devoid of all morality. Those who genuinely love and are willing to help are looked upon as haters who do not love or care about the well-being of others.

If anyone suffers from urges to unite with another person of the same sex, they should not hesitate to denounce the false feelings out loud. If one prevails in losing the self from these false feelings and denounces those spirits while binding Jesus Christ to the soul, he or she will escape captivity, and freedom will flow into the soul.

Adultery

Adultery is sexual intercourse between a married person and another who is not his or her spouse, breaking the vow of the marriage covenant made with his or her spouse. When a husband and wife unite, their souls fuse together, and each person embodies the other. In a situation where the sanctity of this union is broken by an infidel, portals are open for adulterous spirits and spirit husbands and wives to disrupt the matrimonial homes. Mark 10:8 says, "And the two shall become one flesh. So, they are no longer two but one flesh" (ESV).

Spiritually, couples are united and become one. It is essential to seek the face of God as to who to marry and eliminate the chances of adultery. Many people, including great men and women of God, marry but end up with divorce because they did not yield their desires to God so that He could direct them to the right partner. Joining with the wrong spouse allows the enemy to take advantage of an unstable union by tempting one of the spouses to commit adultery.

One should never be ignorant of the vices of the enemy. God created human beings and gave His commandments and laws to guide their steps in their journey through life. The devil, human beings' enemy, guarantees that humans will stray from these commandments as far as they possibly can be misled. Anything contrary to God's laws is destructive to the human soul.

Part of the man's soul is in the woman, and part of the woman's soul is in the man. Their hearts and minds gradually become one. Thus, each person shares the soul of the partner. If an adulterous partner splits his or her soul among many partners, this creates soul ties with many soul mates instead of one, as God legally instituted. Therefore, a gateway is split open for spirit husbands and wives to creep in and torment the marriage and, subsequently, the broken homes. This is the reason why God commands, "You shall not commit adultery" (Exodus 20:14 ESV).

Many marriages are destroyed because of infidelity. Suppose children are involved in a broken home that suffers from instability. They will directly feel the impact and suffer rejection, lack of parental love, and low self-esteem, setting them on a vulnerable path. Humanity is on a battlefield, and the battle of sexual perversions is fierce. It must be confronted, fought, and won in our thoughts and minds, as the Lord Jesus warns,

> But I say to you that everyone who looks at a woman with lustful intent has already committed adultery with her in his heart. (Matthew 5:28 ESV)

Whatever enters the eyes and ears determines what the heart conceives and makes one believe and act upon. We must remain vigilant!

Fornication

Fornication is sexual intercourse between two people who are not in a marriage relationship. The ceremonial activities and vows required for both individuals are not met before uniting their souls. Parents are the primary and core tool for children's upbringing. When parents opt out of that role in a child's life, it is taken over by the internet, perverted television programs, and peer group influence. This presents a situation in which a child grows into a teenager with little or no advice or knowledge on how to face the challenges that come with puberty, as well as a lack of sex education to guide his or her steps through life.

While parents are preoccupied with work from one job or another, the most crucial aspect of a child's education is ignored. By the time parents realize this and try to get their children on the right path, it is too late. The child presents his or her own life preferences, such as addictions and dating many girls or boys, which is not what the parents intended for the child. Parents are obliged to play their roles because an account will be given before God regarding how parents took care of the souls He entrusted to them. Lack of parental care exposes many children to an aberrant lifestyle, such as early sexual involvement. When God created Adam and Eve, He wedded them as husband and wife before pronouncing a blessing of fruitfulness upon them.

> Therefore, a man shall leave his father and his mother and hold fast to his wife, and they shall become one flesh. (Genesis 2:24 ESV)

Whether or not a man and a woman live under the same roof, if they get involved in sexual relations, fornication is committed because they are not held in the bond of marriage. The soul of a young adult who starts dating early in his or her teens is split, depending on how many dating relationships result in sexual intercourse for him or her. The more the soul is split among many dating partners, the greater the number of soul ties, and the more significant the influence of seductive spirits and spirit wives and husbands in his or her life. These soul mates or soul ties result in multiple personalities. The evil one deceives many to get involved in premarital intercourse because there is a greater chance of committing an abortion if a pregnancy occurs, making a bad situation worse.

Many refuse to listen to the call of God's voice in their hearts. We call this voice within us our conscience. If God persists in getting us on the right track in life, and we keep ignoring and resisting His voice, then the following happens:

> This is why God lifted off his restraining hand and let them have full expression of their sinful and shameful desires. They were given over to moral depravity, dishonoring their bodies by sexual perversion among themselves—all because they traded the truth of God for a lie. They worshiped and served the things God made rather than the God who made all things—glory, and praises to him forever and ever! Amen! (Romans 1:24–25 TPT)

The more one surrenders to sexual immorality, the more he or she becomes morally depraved. The only reason why God walked the earth was to direct individuals on their spiritual paths. The Lord Jesus created us for His purpose. The reason for human existence on this earth is for spiritual growth in God. Humans are made of spirit, soul, and body. The spirit births the physical; thus, the spirit is superior and is the priority.

Another adverse effect of premarital intercourse is the lust of one's vision. A good example is the story of Samson, who could not focus and accomplish the call of God that was entrusted to him, as illustrated in Judges 14:1–3 (AMP):

> Samson went down to Timnah, and at Timnah, he saw a woman, one of the daughters of the Philistines. So he went back and told his father and his mother, "I saw a woman in Timnah, one of the daughters of the Philistines; now get her for me as a wife." But his father and mother said to him, "Is there no woman among the daughters of your relatives, or among all our people, that you must go to take a wife from the uncircumcised, pagan Philistines?" And Samson said to his father, "Get her for me because she looks pleasing to me."

Samson's parents were concerned about his union with a pagan Philistine because the state of her soul would directly affect his. If one unites with a wicked and sinful person, the fusion of the souls during intercourse will cause the other to share in the wicked and sinful personality of the other.

Every activity that individuals undertake determines the atmospheric environment surrounding them. Where God's Word and commandments are diligently practiced, the atmosphere is peaceful and filled with God's presence and His holy angels. The virtues of faith are practiced, characterized by loving God above all, good deeds, a kind heart toward others, love among community members, forgiving one another, and loving one's neighbor as oneself, and so forth. On the other hand, when individuals are rebellious to the laws and commandments of God, their atmospheric surroundings are polluted with principalities and demons. Life is a struggle, characterized by the slaughtering of the unborn, lies, corruption, deceit, sexual immorality of all sorts, premature deaths, accidents, natural disasters, wars, unrest, all sorts of violence, and so forth.

There is no situation, however, that our God cannot change and no circumstance too bad for Him to reverse, if we return to Him.

Chapter 8

Come to Me, All You Who Are Weary and Burdened

Just as the voice of John the Baptist cried out in the wilderness, calling all to repent and turn their hearts to the Lord Jesus, the voices of God's messengers continue the cry and call all to repentance from every corner of our world today. All victims are called to bring the burdens of abortion, homosexuality, fornication, adultery, and all sins against the temple of the Holy Spirit laid upon our souls by the evil one to the Lord Jesus Christ and cast them unto Him.

The battle of sin is fought in a person's mind. What goes on in a person's mind is what the person believes. And what a person believes is what he or she practices because he or she believes it to be accurate and correct.

At times, we know very well that something is wrong but we don't have the willpower to do what is right. An example is when the apostle Paul said that he is a mystery to himself, for he wants to do what is right but ends up doing what his moral instincts condemn. And if his behavior is not in line with his desire, his conscience still confirms the excellence of the Law. And he realizes that it is no longer his true self doing it but the unwelcome intruder of sin in his humanity. For he knows that nothing good lives within the flesh of fallen humanity.

The longings to do what is right are within him, but willpower is not enough to accomplish it. His lofty desires to do what is good are dashed when he does what he wants to avoid. So if his behavior contradicts his desires to do good, he must conclude that it's not his true identity doing it but the unwelcome intruder of sin, hindering him from being who he really is (Romans 7:15–20).

This presents an awareness that only the power in the perfect blood of our Lord Jesus can undo the fallen and imperfect DNA in human blood. We must understand that our true identities are found in Him alone, and through His grace, we have the ability to resist and conquer sin.

The Lord Jesus dictates in His sermon,

> Therefore, do not allow your hearts to turn to stone or to be overgrown with weeds and thistles. Keep them at all times ready so that My Word, which reanimates your soul in so many different ways, can sprout therein. so you do not have to share the fate of those who accept My Word only superficially and, when it requires action, prove that the seed had clung only to the surface of their heart but had not penetrated it at all.[6]

---

[6] Gottfried Mayerhofer, "The Parable of the Sower," Eleventh Sermon of Jesus (January 20, 1872).

The Lord further calls us to humble our hearts before Him:

> If my people who are called by my name humble themselves and pray and seek my face and turn from their wicked ways, then I will hear from heaven and will forgive their sin and heal their land. (2 Chronicles 7:14 ESV)

Sin may play its role in staining our souls, but the precious blood of the Lord Jesus overcomes all sin. There is no stain of sin that His blood cannot eliminate. He who created all vessels will restore all His broken vessels. Our Lord, through His blood, makes us anew. For this reason, while on the Mount of Olives, the Lord Jesus told His disciples to call men to repentance and draw them all to Him, as He said,

> O my brethren and friends, sons of the father who has chosen you from all men, you know that I have often told you that I must be crucified and must die for the salvation of Adam and his posterity and that I should rise from the dead. Now I shall commit to you the doctrine of the Holy Gospel formally announced to you, that you may declare it throughout the whole world. And I shall endow you with power from on high and fill you with the Holy Spirit. Luke 24:49. And you shall declare, to all nations, repentance and remission of sins. Luke 24:37. For a single cup of water, Matt 10:42 for man shall find it, and the world to come is greater and better than all the wealth of this whole world. And as much ground as one foot can occupy in my father's house is greater and more excellent than all the earth's riches. Yea, a single hour in the joyful dwelling of the pious is more blessed and more precious than a thousand years amongst sinners. Inasmuch as there

is weeping, and lamentation shall not come to an end, their tears shall not cease, nor shall they find for themselves consolation and repose for any time forever. And now, O my honored members, go declare to all nations. Tell them and say to them, verily, the savior diligently inquires into the inheritance which is due and is the administrator of justice.[7]

Many aimed to acquire and preserve wealth, adapt, and live in sin. But the Lord illustrates in the above passage that wealth, which can provide neither good health nor peace of mind, is what beautifies this sinful world. But a glance of the world to come, however, surpasses all the wealth. The world to come is defined by God's presence and is full of His glory. The Spirit of God comes with the spirit of wisdom, the spirit of knowledge, the spirit of understanding, the spirit of the fear of the Lord, and two other spirits. The mentioned spirits are essential in guiding our paths on the earth. Given that sin veils the presence of God, those living in sinfulness are deprived of these fruits brought by the presence of God's spirit, resulting in their depraved minds. For this is the reason, the Lord Jesus never stops summoning us to turn our burdens to Him:

You have entrusted me with all that you are and all that you have. No one fully and intimately knows the Son except the father. And no one fully and intimately knows the Father except the Son. But the Son is able to unveil the Father to anyone he chooses. Are you weary, carrying a heavy burden? Come to me. I will refresh your life, for I am your oasis. Simply join your life with mine. Learn my

---

[7] Alexander Roberts, "The History of Joseph the Carpenter," *The Fathers of the Church*.

ways, and you'll discover that I'm gentle, humble, easy to please. You will find refreshment and rest in me. (Matthew 11:27–29 TPT)

In the same way that Jesus stood before me like a mountain in a vision—hard to get close because I was distracted by blasphemers—so does sin sway us away from our God. When we turn our gaze and focus on Him, the Lord comes close to us and walks by our side as a close friend.

To be in Jesus is the only way through which our invisible battles can be fought and won. Let us turn to our Creator and cast off the burdens of sin and spiritual battles upon Him. Get rid of oppression and suffering brought about by the lifestyle reminiscent of Sodom and Gomorrah. Draw close to God, and let Him take over the battle.

> Draw near to God, and he will draw near to you. Cleanse your hands, you sinners, and purify your hearts, you double-minded. (James 4:8 ESV).

As we surrender all to the Lord Jesus, we will continue to walk in obedience and follow in the footsteps of our Lord and Savior Jesus Christ and let Him take over the war. Given that the war is the Lord's, we have no need to fear.

> And he said, "Listen, all Judah and inhabitants of Jerusalem and King Jehoshaphat: Thus, says the Lord to you, 'Do not be afraid and do not be dismayed at this great horde, for the battle is not yours but God's.'" (2 Chronicles 20:15 ESV)

God stands with everyone who looks up to Him and does His will. We wrestle not against our fellow brothers and sisters in the flesh but against principalities and powers of the air that influence our lives, as the apostle Paul wrote in his message to the Ephesians, explaining why the armor we put on is not man's but God's.

Retrieve the Blessings

As we return to our Lord and Savior Jesus Christ, we also embark on the journey to take back all that the devil has stolen from us. We start by renouncing and losing from our souls all false feelings and lies of the evil one and by getting baptized and being rooted and firm in our walk with God. We also make sure our lives are characterized by meditating on God's Word, worshipping, praising, being prayerful, and waiting on the Lord, while, at the same time, shutting our eyes and ears to the biased and perverted media outlets and casting down anything that exalts itself above the knowledge of God.

We must keep in mind that the devil will not let go easily or quickly. But we also must be mindful of the Word that says, "So then, surrender to God. Stand up to the devil and resist him, and he will flee in agony" (James 4:7 TPT).

All blessings from God, such as children, promotions, financial blessings, and, most importantly, spiritual growth that gives life to the soul now enter our coffers and not the devil's coffers. For instance, if we are faced with a circumstance whereby we are supposed to speak the truth, but we choose to tell lies to protect ourselves, the blessing we are supposed to receive from overcoming evil and embracing truth is stolen by the evil spirit of lies. This is how the devil, the thief, steals our blessings. We must maintain the notion that anything against the commandments of God is the devil's tool, used to steal God's protection from us and prevent us from abstaining from sin and overcoming him.

All evil has no solid ground and cannot last. In the book of Matthew 4:11, it is written, "Then the devil left him, and behold, angels came and were ministering to him" (ESV).

After the devil's unsuccessful three attempts to push the Lord Jesus into sin, heavenly angels came and ministered to Him. Whenever we triumph over the temptations of the evil one, the holy angels of God come and minister to us. We receive the price of our victory, and the more we continue to overcome evil and reclaim our blessings, the more our lives transform. We develop spiritually, cultivating the treasured gifts of the spirit invested in us by our Lord Jesus Christ. Pain and suffering are abolished, and we live a life worthy of being called sons and daughters of God.

No matter what we have gone through in life, one truth stands: God's love for us cannot be measured. He loves us so much that He had to step into human flesh and die for us, as He said:

> For the greatest love of all is a love that sacrifices all. And this great love is demonstrated when a person sacrifices his life for his friends. (John 15:13 TPT)

He did not do it for a particular group of people and leave some out. No! He came and died for *all*. No two persons on earth exist with the same fingerprints. That tells us how unique and essential every single person is to Him. The Lord Jesus Christ stands waiting—and has always been waiting—with wide open arms, waiting for every single one of us to step out of the lies and deceptions of the evil one and come running to His embrace, bury our heads on His chest, and feel the warmth of the Father's love.

Know that Jesus Christ, our Creator, loves us so much that *nothing* can come between us and His love for us! Kindly pray the following brief prayer if you want to give your life to the Lord Jesus and become a member of God's family:

Heavenly Father, I believe that You sent Your only begotten Son to die on the cross for me, and You raised Him from the dead on the third day. Lord Jesus, I renounce and repent of all my sins, and I accept You as my personal Lord and Savior. I believe that through the shedding of Your blood, all my sins are washed away. Lord, I surrender my life into Your hands now. Please come into my heart and make Your home in me.

Printed in the United States
by Baker & Taylor Publisher Services